LITERARY CHAMPION

STUDY COMPANION FOR LITERATURE

NAVEEN SHARMA

Contents

Preface

This book has been written as a source to provide students and readers of this book, all the necessary information about all important literary elements, forms, definitions, devices and background information which would be useful for you to have a clear idea about literary creations. It also carries ways and suggestions to write critical analysis for the convenience of the students with little or no experience of studying English literature. All aspects of literature which have inscribed in this book have been shown and discussed in a clear and concise way to give an easy and understandable experience to the students. In last portion of the book you will learn about patter of writing answers for questions of different kinds and conditions.

Salient Features

- Comprehensive language
- Background information
- Detailed description
- Ways and suggestions
- Questions and answers

ONE

LITERARY TERMS AND FORMS

Allusion

An allusion is when an author refers to the events or characters from another story in his own story with the hope that those events will add context or depth to the story which he is trying to tell to the readers. For example, one of the most alluded to texts in literature is the Bible and specially the New Testament.

Genre in literature

A literary genre is a category or form of literary compositions. Genres may be determined by literary technique, tone, content, even length and rhyme. Types: Drama, poetry, non-fiction, fiction, prose, etc.

Symbolism

It is the practice or art of using an object or a word to represent an abstract idea. An action, person, place, word or object can have a systematic meaning.

In literature, symbolism can take many forms including:

A figure of speech where an object, person or situation has another meaning other than its literary meaning.

The actions of a character, word, action or event that has a deeper meaning in the context of the whole story.

Imagery

Imagery in a literary text, is an author's use of vivid and descriptive language to add depth to the work. It appeals and gives chance to human senses to deepen the reader's understanding of the work. Powerful form of imagery engages all of the senses.

Allegory

As a literary device, It is a metaphor in which a character, place or event is used to deliver a broader message about real world issues.

Setting

The setting of a piece of literature is the time and place in which the story takes place. The definition of setting can also include social statuses, weather, historical period, and details about immediate surroundings. Settings can be real or fictional, or a combination of both real and fictional elements. Some settings are very specific (Wulfhall in Wiltshire England in 1500), while others are descriptive (a boat out on the ocean). Most pieces of literature include more—or many more—than one setting, either as the narrative progresses through time or to include points of view from more than one character.

Tone

In literature, tone is the attitude or approach that the author takes toward the work's central theme or subject. Works of literature can have many different types of tone, such as humorous, solemn, distant, intimate, ironic, arrogant, condescending, sentimental, and so on. Any emotion that humans can feel can be an example of tone in literature.

Difference between Tone and Mood

Tone and mood are very often confused. While definition of tone is the attitude the author has toward the work, the mood consists of the feelings the work produces in an audience or reader. Authors use tone as well as setting, theme, and voice to produce a certain mood. In cinema directors can add the use of music, editing, and images to help create mood. For example, horror movies almost always include suspenseful and anxiety-producing music. If, instead, bright jazz music were playing while a character is in danger, the audience would not feel the mood of suspense.

Wring style

A writing style is **an author's unique way of communicating with words**. An author creates a style with the voice, or personality, and overall tone that they apply to their text. A writer's style can change depending on the type of writing they're doing, who they're writing for, and their target audience.

Types

- Expository writing
- Descriptive writing
- Persuasive writing
- Narrative writing
- Creative writing

Roman a clef

A novel that tells a loosely disguised true story, using fictional names for the characters, can be called a roman a clef. Sometimes it can also be used in poems for the same purpose.

Motif

Motif is an object or idea that repeats itself throughout a literary work.

Motif and Theme

In a literary work, a motif can be seen as an image, sound, action, or other figures that has a symbolic significance, and contributes toward the development of a theme. Motif and theme are linked in a literary work, but there is a difference between them. In a literary piece, a motif is a recurrent image, idea, or symbol that develops or explains a theme, while a theme is a central idea or message. Theme can be divided in two categories: a work's thematic concept is what readers think about the work is about and, thematic statement being, what the work says about the subject.

Motif and Symbol

Sometimes, examples of motifs are mistakenly identified as examples of symbols. Symbols are images, ideas, sounds, or words that represent something else, and help to understand an idea or a thing. Motifs, on the other hand, are images, ideas, sounds, or words that help to explain the central idea of a literary work – the theme. Moreover, a symbol may appear once or twice in a literary work, whereas a motif is a recurring element.

Conflict in literature

In literature, conflict is a literary element that involves a struggle between two opposing forces, usually a protagonist and an antagonist.

Internal Conflict

1. **Mind vs. Body:** One type of internal conflict that occurs in stories is mind versus body. It occurs when the protagonist or the main character fights against his bodily addiction such as in the case of some drug addict. Some may fight against the religious belief that has proved wrong or against political dogmas such as in Animal Farm.

2. **Mind vs. Mind:** The second internal conflict is mind versus mind which is the mental thinking conflict. It occurs when a person has desires but he also has to fulfill his responsibilities. He has to perform his duty as well as do his responsibility or commit suicide and die or struggle for his survival. This is called mind versus mind conflict as it happens in Frankenstein by Mary Shelley.

- **Mind vs. Reality:** Some literary works present worlds that do not match with reality such as the dystopian world of The Handmaid's Tale created by Margret Atwood, the world of magical realism created by Garcia Marquez, or the world created by the superiority complex or right versus just people. This is called mind versus reality conflict.

External Conflict

1. **Conflict with Nature:** It happens when a man comes into conflict with nature. It happens in Hardy's novels as his protagonist comes into conflict with nature and loses such. Another example is Santiago of Hemingway in the Old Man and the Sea.
2. **Conflict with Another Person:** This conflict happens with the thinking and subsequent actions of the people that do not match and create a conflict between them. Happens in Tess of D'Urberville by Thomas Hardy that she has a conflict with Alec and then with Angel.
3. **Conflict with Society:** It happens with the main protagonist comes into conflict with the social setup, norms, traditions, and conventions. It happens in Tess of

D'Urberville of Thomas Hardy that she breaks the social norms of those times.

Core Conflict

As a novel or a play has several characters, events, and situations, there are numerous conflicts at play. They also move side by side and keep the readers and audiences engaged. However, there is only one principal character or protagonist who comes into conflict with the outside world, society, or nature and creates maximum tension and suspense. This is called the core conflict whose resolution is central to the world of literary piece such as Michael Henchard in The Mayor of Casterbridge by Thomas Hardy.

Character Conflict

This conflict occurs only due to the characters and their interactions. When one character does not find it easy to sync his interests with that of the others and faces obstacles, this creates a conflict between the characters. This is called character conflict. It happens in The Kite Runner by Khalid Hosseini.

Conflict and Plot

Conflict is one of the most important elements of the plot. As the plot is the larger world, conflict is its critical part. If there is no conflict, it means the plot has lost a critical component and may not have a good storyline. Missing conflict means missing the resolution. So, the readers would not be able to hold any interest in the plot or storyline having no conflict.

Elements of Conflict

1. **Misunderstandings:** Conflict occurs due to misunderstanding between two parties or characters or man and nature, man and another person, or even man and society.
2. **Differences in Values and Beliefs:** This entails both external as well as internal conflicts within a person or even between different persons. However, the major issues occur over values and beliefs.
3. **Differences in Interest:** This occurs due to different interests and clashes between those interests. The characters come into conflict due to this clash.
4. **Interpersonal Differences:** Interpersonal differences also cause a conflict between characters.
5. **Feelings and Emotions:** This conflict occurs due to the differences between the feelings and emotions of different characters.

Difference between Conflict and Tension in Literature

Conflict is a serious tense situation between characters due to some dispute, squabble, or controversy. However, tension does not simply mean that it is due to some dispute. It is just an impending sense of something ominous that is about to happen but may not happen even until the end. It could be the fear of divorce, the sense of disclosure or some secret that may cause a rift among the characters, or even the discovery of something that continue to haunt the characters.

What does Conflict Mean in a Story?

Conflict in a story means that the characters are interacting with each other and one another and that they have good or bad relations to build their lives on. The existence of a conflict in the story means the progress of the story. It takes the story to the next level as it prompts the characters to do something and not sit idle. Therefore, conflict is as important in the story as characters, situations, and settings.

What is the Central Conflict or Core Conflict?

A story or a narrative could have several conflicts in case there are several characters or events. However, there is the main conflict that runs throughout the story until the end. This is called the central conflict or the core conflict upon which the success of the story hinges. Besides this conflict, there could be several small or minor conflicts going on between secondary characters, foils, or minor characters.

Function of Conflict

Both internal and external conflicts are essential elements of a storyline. It is essential for a writer to introduce and develop them, whether internal, external, or both, in his storyline in order to achieve the story's goal. Resolution of the conflict entertains the readers.

Rising action

Rising action in a plot is a series of relevant incidents that create suspense, interest, and tension in a narrative. In literary works, a rising action includes all decisions, characters' flaws, and background circumstances that together create turns and twists leading to a climax. We find it in novels, plays, and short stories. Rising action is one of the elements of plot, which begins immediately after its exposition.

Exposition

Exposition is a literary device that is designed to convey important information, within a short story or novel, to the reader. Writers utilize exposition to provide essential backstory for characters, plot, and other narrative elements. This background information allows the reader of a story to emotionally invest in the narrative's arc, characters, and action. Exposition also enhances the reader's understanding of a literary work and encourages their connection to it.

Climax

The climax in a short story is **the turning point where the protagonist confronts the main conflict, creating the most intense moment.**

Falling Action

Falling action refers to **the events that follow the climax of a story**. While rising action builds tension throughout the story, falling action decreases that tension. It leads to the character's ultimate resolution.

Resolution

The resolution is **the end of the story**. It occurs after the Climax. It is when you learn what happens to the characters after the Conflict is resolved.

Fare shadowing

Foreshadowing is a literary device that writers utilize as a means to indicate or hint to readers something that is to follow or appear later in a story. Foreshadowing, when done properly, is an excellent device in terms of creating suspense and dramatic tension for readers. It can set up emotional expectations of character behaviors and/or plot outcomes. This can heighten a reader's enjoyment of a literary work, enhance the work's meaning, and help the reader make connections with other literature and literary themes.

Ways

- Character dialogues
- Plot events
- Changes in setting

Prologue vs. Epilogue

A prologue is an independent front matter of the novel, which gives an opening hint to the reader, as to what the story is all about. On the contrary, an epilogue implies a literary device, which is an additional and independent part of the literary work, which concludes the story.

Soliloquy vs. Monologue

A soliloquy is a long speech spoken by a single character that is not intended to be heard by any other character in the play. A monologue is spoken by a single character but is addressed to the other characters on stage.

Pastoral poem

A pastoral poetry type is a type of poetry that depicts rural life in a peaceful, idealized way for examples of shepherds or country life.

Satire

Satire is a technique employed by writers to expose and criticize foolishness and corruption of an individual or a society by using humor, irony, exaggeration or ridicule. It intends to improve humanity by criticizing its follies and foibles. A writer in satire uses fictional characters which stand for real people to expose and condemn their corruption. A writer may point a satire towards a person, a country, or even the entire world. In simple terms, it's a great example for the use of wit.

Satire and Irony (Interlinked)

Irony is the difference between what is said or done, and what is actually meant. Therefore, writers frequently employ satire to point at the dishonesty and silliness of individuals and society, and criticize them by ridiculing them.

Eulogy

A eulogy is a speech or writing done to praise a person, and his life. They are often given at funerals.

Ode

An ode is a special kind of poem, usually praising something. It is a form of lyrical poetry- expressing emotion and it is usually addressed to someone or something, or it represents the poet's musings on that person or thing. Usually it's not too lengthy. The poet who used Ode very well or we can say in the best way is John Keats, it had a specific structure.

Ballad

This is a kind of poem that is typically arranged in quatrains with rhyme pattern of ABAB. These are usually narrative and often about love.

Invocation

It is defined as the act of appealing to a higher authority for help. It is a formal prayer to the muses for inspiration, help and guidance at the beginning of an epic.

Sonnets in literature

A sonnet is a specific type of poem that consists 14 lines and is written in Iambic pentameter. In literature there are two types of sonnets:

- Petrarchan (Italian) sonnet
- Shakespearean (English) sonnet

The type of sonnet is identifies by its rhyming scheme and affiliated aspects.

What is Iambic pentameter?

Each line of a sonnet is divided into 10 syllables and 5 Iambs. In poetry, a pair of syllables is also called a foot. An iamb is a special pair of syllables, one unstressed and other stressed. This flowing from unstressed to stressed syllables is called Iambic pentameter in action.

Petrarchan (Italian) Sonnet

The Petrarchan (named after the 14th century Italian poet Francesco Petrarch) or Italian sonnet has an octave of 8 lines followed by a sestet of 6 lines. The octet and sestet have their own rhyming schemes.

The most common patterns for the octet are abbaabba and abbacddc. The sestet has pattern of either defdef or dedede.

Shakespearean (English) Sonnet

Another important category of sonnet is the English sonnet. As we can see in the name, this form was used by him, though it was not created by him. This kind of sonnet is totally different from Petrarchan sonnet in both its rhyming scheme and structure.

These are divided into three quatrains of four lines each one followed by a couplet of two lines. And unlike previous sonnet, it has a rhyme pattern of abab, cdcd, efef, gg.

The final couplet is used to summarize the previous 12 lines or present a surprise ending.

Epic vs. Mock Epic

An epic is a long work in poetry that usually reveals the story of a hero and his struggles and heroic incidents. There is usually a journey and many great battles. It is usually written Dactylic hexameter.

On the other hand, a mock epic poetry is something that may have the feel of an epic but content is pointedly not heroic. Mock-epic draws heavily on the technique of satire, which means that it usually uses irony, exaggeration and sarcasm for creating humor to mock its original subject in a very undignified and grandiose manner. In English literature, John Dryden's "Mac-Flecknoe" is considered as greatest mock-epic poetry ever. The both epic and mock-epic may have invocation as well in beginning.

What is Dactylic Hexameter?

It is also called heroic hexameter and the meter of heroic. It is a form of meter or rhyming scheme in poetry. Hexameter is usually six feet per line.

Poem vs. Poetry

Poetry is the use of words, language and the process of creating a literary piece using metaphor, simile and symbols to evoke a writer's feelings and thoughts, while a poem is the final result and arrangement of words.

TWO

TRAGEDY VS. COMEDY

Tragedy is a genre of drama based on human suffering and, mainly, the terrible or sorrowful events that befall a main character. Traditionally, the intention of tragedy is to invoke an accompanying catharsis, or a pain that awakens pleasure, for the audience. In literature, it is a composition that describes a series of misfortunes in the lives of the main characters that bring them to ruin as the consequence of a tragic flaw, weakness of character or adverse circumstances.

Comedy isa literary genre and a type of dramatic work that is amusing and satirical in its tone, mostly having a cheerful ending. The motif of this dramatic work is triumph over unpleasant circumstance by creating comic effects, resulting in a happy or successful conclusion. Its purpose is to amuse the audience. (Tragedy is opposite to comedy as it deals with the sorrowful and tragic events in a story.)

Types of Comedy

- Romantic comedy
- Comedy of humors
- Comedy of manners
- Sentimental comedy
- Tragicomedy

Sub genres of comedy

- Farce
- Satire
- Burlesque

What is Humor?

It is a tool that makes audience laugh, or that intends to induce, amusement or laughter.

What is Melodrama?

It is a creative performance or actions with lots of pretended and exaggerated emotion, tension or excitement.

What is Tragicomedy?

A play or novel containing elements of both comedy and tragedy. Mostly, the characters in it are exaggerated and sometimes there might be a happy ending after a series of unfortunate events. It is incorporated with jokes throughout the story, just to lighten the tone.

What is the significance of comic interludes?

Literally, comic interludes are known as tragic relief. A tragedy creates tension in the mind of the audience. Therefore, it is necessary to relax the minds of the audience by including comic scenes in the play, otherwise, it generates some sort of emotional weakness. Because of being a branch of comedy, tragic relief can be also known as comic relief. In any literary work, it is an author's use of humor to give the readers or audience an emotional break from the tension and heavy mood of serious and tragic plot. This can include humorous characters, clever dialogues, and funny scenes.

What is tragic flaw?

It is a literary device that can be defined as a trait in a character leading to his downfall, and the character is often the hero of literary piece. This trait can be the lack of self-knowledge, lack of the decision making and often is pride. A tragic flaw is also called a "Fatal flaw" in literature and films. This is taken as a defective trait in the character of the hero.

What is the function and purpose of tragic flaw?

It is used for moral purposes in order to encourage the audience to improve their characters and remove the flaws which can bring their downfall in life. The readers and audience can identify themselves with tragic hero, since it imparts feelings of pity and fear among them, thereby completing their catharsis or in other words- they are purged of bad emotions. Therefore, they can learn a moral lesson so that they might not indulge in similar actions in future.

What is catharsis?

It is known as the purification of emotions, related to intense feelings of pity and fear. The effect of such kind of purification is spiritual renewal.

THREE

GOTHIC LITERATURE

The Rise of Gothic

The first mention of gothic literature was found in English writer Horace Walpole's "The Castle of Otranto" that got published in the year 1764. He applied the word in the subtitle "A Gothic story".

What is Gothic Literature?

It is a genre of literature that emerged as one of the eeriest forms of dark romanticism in late 1700s, which became a rapidly spreading romanticism movement later. Dark romanticism was a period of English Literature that is characterized by expressions of terror, gruesome narratives, supernatural elements and dark picturesque scenery. This fictional genre encompasses many different elements and has undergone impactful a series of revivals since its inception.

Key Elements

- Mystery and fear
- Curses
- Omens
- Atmosphere and setting
- Supernatural and paranormal activity
- Romance
- Villain
- Emotional distress
- Nightmares
- Anti-hero
- Damsel in distress

All these elements give a mysterious and special outlook to the story of any literary creation and give readers a suspenseful condition to arise to arise suspicion excited expectation and uncertainty about what may happen.

FOUR

WHAT IS DICTION?

Diction

The choice and use of words and phrases in the speech or writing is called diction.

Denotation vs. Connotation

Denotation is the actual literal definition or meaning of a word or term. It is also referred as dictionary definition. It gives a more descriptive definition of a term.

While, connotation is an association of a term. It can also be an emotional input attached to a word thus making it more figurative and suggestive, it can have a variety of descriptions on the basis of affiliated factors.

FIVE

CRITICAL ANALYSIS

Critical analysis essays can be a challenging form of the academic writing, but crafting a good critical analysis on paper can be straightforward and easily done task if you have the right approach to observe and compose.

What Is a Critical Analysis Essay?

Critical analysis essays combine the skills of critical reading, critical thinking, and critical writing. In a critical analysis essay, the author considers a piece of literature, a piece of nonfiction, or a work of art and analyzes the author or artist's points. This type of essay focuses on the author's thesis, argument, and point of view by adhering to logical reasoning and offering supporting evidence.

How to Write a Critical Analysis Essay?

The critical analysis process has two key components, each of which is equally important. The first is the reading process. The purpose of a critical analysis assignment is to demonstrate an understanding of your subject matter. This means you carefully read, watch, or otherwise study your source text. The second part is the writing process itself. Below are nine organizational and writing tips to help you craft the best possible critical analysis essay.

1. Read Thoroughly and Carefully.

You will need to accurately represent an author's point of view and techniques. Be sure you truly understand them before you begin the writing process.

2. Choose a Thesis Statement.

Your thesis should make a claim about the author's point of view and writing style. It should present a perspective that you can back up with evidence from the text; remember, the purpose of your essay is to provide analysis of someone else's work. Choose a thesis statement around which you can anchor your entire analytical essay.

3. Write an Introductory Paragraph.

An excellent introduction can engage your reader's interest, so take extra care when writing your opening paragraph. The best introductions often start with a hook such as a rhetorical question or a bold statement. Your intro paragraph must also name the book or work of art that your analysis will tackle. Use the author's name, the title of the work, and any relevant publication information. A good introduction concludes with a thesis statement that serves as the North Star for the entire essay.

4. Carefully Organize the Body of Your Essay.

After your introductory paragraph, divide your essay into body paragraphs that delve into specific topics. All body paragraphs should serve the main goal of supporting your thesis statement, either by providing background information, digging into details, or providing contrasting viewpoints. The number of body paragraphs will vary depending on the scope of your essay. The structure of your essay is just as important as the subject of your essay, so take the time to plan each body paragraph.

5. Craft Clear Topic Sentences.

Each main body paragraph should begin with a topic sentence that offers a brief summary of the forthcoming paragraph and ties it to your main thesis.

6. Populate Your Essay With Evidence.

The main body of the essay should be filled with a mixture of substance and analysis. You won't convince your audience by making statements without solid evidence to back it up. Therefore, support the main points of your analysis with textual evidence taken from your source material. Use footnotes and endnotes as necessary.

7. Summarize Your Analysis in a Concluding Paragraph.

Whether you're aiming for a good grade or just trying to give your audience a satisfying reading experience, wrap up your analytical essay with a concluding paragraph that recaps your argument. The concluding paragraph is not the place to introduce new evidence. Rather, it is the bow on your entire essay, reminding your reader of your most important points and leaving them with some final words for consideration.

8. Revise as Necessary.

Once you've finished a draft, set it down for a few hours or a few days and come back to proofread it with fresh eyes. Ask yourself the following questions: Am I accurately representing the author's point of view? Am I backing up my assertions with evidence from the text? Am I providing analysis rather than my own personal opinion? Are my sentences clear, my grammar correct, and my spelling accurate?

9. Write a Final Draft.

Based on your self-analysis in the prior step, edit your essay to implement the needed changes. At this point, you can consider your essay ready to submit—or, feel free to show it to a friend, teacher, or mentor for a fresh perspective on your work.

In simple terms, we can understand critical analysis by following ways:

- Ask question from yourself
- Collect evidence
- Construct thesis

- Develop and organize arguments
- Write the introduction
- Write the body paragraph
- Write the conclusion

SIX

HOW TO WRITE LITERARY ANSWERS?

Key points of a good answer:

a. Introduction
b. Main body
c. Conclusion

We can use these following relevant points to write the brief and detailed answers:

Condition 1: If question is about writer only.

- Author's country
- The age to which he belonged
- His favorite genre as author
- His most famous works
- Any prominent incident or information of his life and his contemporary writers.
- Take reference of his any creation which is part of your syllabus to make a critical view about him.
- What critics said about him?
- Dominant literary trends of his period.
- Any awards won by him
- Writers who got influenced by him and what we think about him as a critical reader.
- Key elements of literary works like themes, imagery, motif, etc.

Condition 2: If question is about critical analysis.

Introduction

- Glimpse of question
- Historical background related to the content
- Introduction about author
- Genre of the text

Main body

- Sequence of most relevant incidents and their critical analysis in a critical manner.
- What did critics comment about the text?
- Discuss main themes of the text.
- Tell the mystery about which the whole text revolves,
- Either criticize or appreciate writer's work by taking reference by of the text with having evidence of thesis.

Conclusion

- Give a final opinion about the text without being double sided.
- Mention any other critic too who also commented same about the text as a reference behind your answer in order to justify if needed.

Condition 3: If question is about poem only.

- Start with the topic or issue asked in the question.
- Write poetic genre of the poem and justify your statement.
- Critically examine poet's poetic style with reference of that poem.
- Historical background of the poem and poet.
- Write literary devices which used in poem by poet with examples.
- Write opinions of critics who commented about the poem.

- Compare poem of question with the literary trends of the period in which poem was written.
- Give a final opinion in last with an explanatory note.

Condition 4: If question is about character analysis.

- Introduction to the character
- Information about the text in which the character belongs.
- Discuss the role of character in the text.
- Write key points of his characters with the help of incidents in the text which justify your views.
- Opinions of critics about characters.
- What were the mistakes done by him which ruined his life or what were that good decisions which made his life better?
- Make a final judgement of the character in last.

Key points of a good answer:

a. Introduction
b. Main body
c. Conclusion

We can use these following relevant points to write the brief and detailed answers:

Condition 1: If question is about writer only.

We can use these relevant points to write the brief and detailed answers:

- Author's country
- The age to which he belonged
- His favorite genre as author
- His most famous works
- Any prominent incident or information of his life and his contemporary writers.
- Take reference of his any creation which is part of your syllabus to make a critical view about him.
- What critics said about him?
- Dominant literary trends of his period.
- Any awards won by him
- Writers who got influenced by him and what we think about him as a critical reader.
- Key elements of literary works like themes, imagery, motif, etc.

Condition 2: If question is about critical analysis.
Introduction

- Glimpse of question
- Historical background related to the content
- Introduction about author
- Genre of the text

Main body

- Sequence of most relevant incidents and their critical analysis in a critical manner.
- What did critics comment about the text?
- Discuss main themes of the text.
- Tell the mystery about which the whole text revolves,
- Either criticize or appreciate writer's work by taking reference by of the text with having evidence of thesis.

Conclusion

- Give a final opinion about the text without being double sided.
- Mention any other critic too who also commented same about the text as a reference behind your answer in order to justify if needed.

Condition 3: If question is about poem only.

- Start with the topic or issue asked in the question.
- Write poetic genre of the poem and justify your statement.
- Critically examine poet's poetic style with reference of that poem.
- Historical background of the poem and poet.
- Write literary devices which used in poem by poet with examples.
- Write opinions of critics who commented about the poem.
- Compare poem of question with the literary trends of the period in which poem was written.
- Give a final opinion in last with an explanatory note.

Condition 4: If question is about character analysis.

- Introduction to the character
- Information about the text in which the character belongs.
- Discuss the role of character in the text.
- Write key points of his characters with the help of incidents in the text which justify your views.
- Opinions of critics about characters.

- What were the mistakes done by him which ruined his life or what were that good decisions which made his life better?
- Make a final judgement of the character in last.

9 798887 831312

Printed by Libri Plureos GmbH in Hamburg,
Germany